Wonderful Things

belongs to
Michelle Graabek

By learning you will teach
By teaching you will learn
Latin proverb

Acknowledgements

This book was originally made possible with funding from the UK's Museums, Libraries and Archives Council (MLA).

Particular thanks is due to Jan Horrell at the MLA for her assistance, and to all staff and volunteers at The Museum of Barnstaple & North Devon, especially Alison Mills and Melanie Terrell. Thanks also to the team involved in the creation of the Think Tank system.

Wonderful Things

Learning with Museum Objects

Julian Vayne

MUSEUMSETC | EDINBURGH & BOSTON

Contents

About This Book

At first I could see nothing, the hot air escaping from the chamber causing the candle flame to flicker, but presently, as my eyes grew accustomed to the light, details of the room within emerged slowly from the mist, strange animals, statues, and gold – everywhere the glint of gold. For the moment – an eternity it must have seemed to the others standing by – I was struck dumb with amazement, and when Lord Carnarvon, unable to stand the suspense any longer, inquired anxiously, "Can you see anything?" it was all I could do to get out the words, "Yes, wonderful things." – Howard Carter, on opening the tomb of Tutankhamen.

This is a book about wonderful things. From rare artefacts cherished within museum collections, through to found objects discovered at your local car boot sale. This book grows from the simple fact that learning by engaging with objects can be a powerful experience. Whether you are a school teacher, a museum professional, a learner, or simply intrigued by this method of teaching, there will be something here for you.

This book is written in a straightforward style, in which I've tried to minimise the amount of either museum or educational jargon. Part of the reason for this is that learning with objects is something that can happen in a variety of situations (youth clubs, home school groups, day centres for older people and many more). However, to keep the text simple I'm going to assume that the objects we are talking about are from a museum collection and are being used in a conventional school setting.

The first section of this book explores the background to working with objects. The second part will provide you with a wide variety of games and ideas that you can use. Each game is printed on a separate page so that you can make your own notes about them. Please think of this book as a manual of techniques; adapt, explore and amend the ideas presented here to suit your own style and situation.

LEARNING

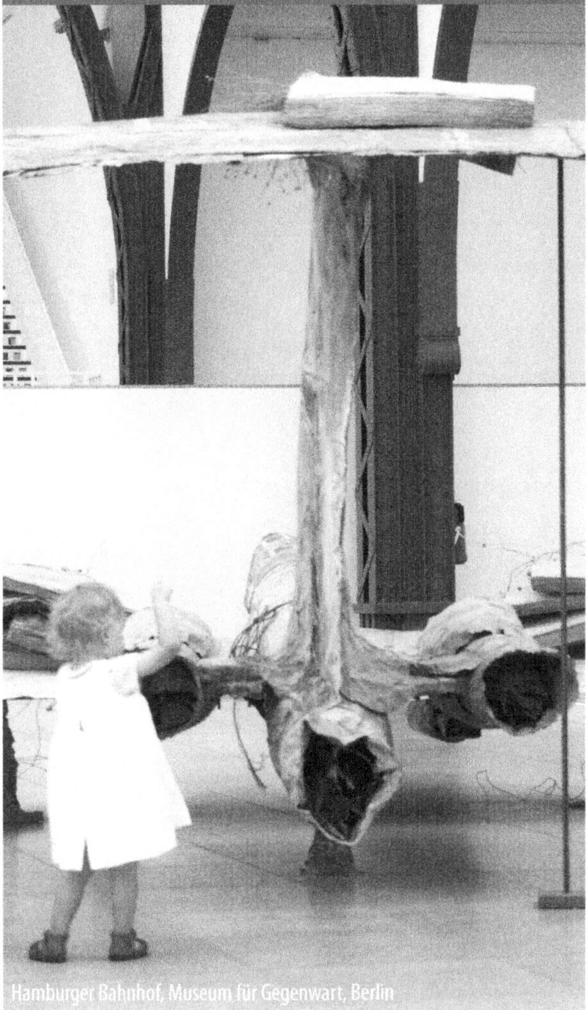

Hamburger Bahnhof, Museum für Gegenwart, Berlin

Learning from Objects

What is an object? We could be talking about a natural history specimen, a flint arrowhead, a World War II air-raid precaution warden's helmet, or perhaps a 3.5-inch floppy disk. These objects could come from a museum collection, be sourced from an archive, or be discovered in your own home. The word *object* covers all these things neatly. It also allows us to recognise the most important element of the object in that it's "out there", it's a thing in the world, separate from our bodies and maybe far removed from our everyday experience. By exploring different ways of engaging with an object we can learn all kinds of things. This can be both one of the most cognitively rich methods of learning and also one of the most concrete and immediate.

Getting hold of wonderful things

Depending on the nature of the objects you want to work with, and your client group, you will need to negotiate with other stakeholders (of which the museum manager, curator or collections officer will typically be the most important) about which objects are "fair game" for mainstream educational use and which are not.

A balance needs to be struck between protecting

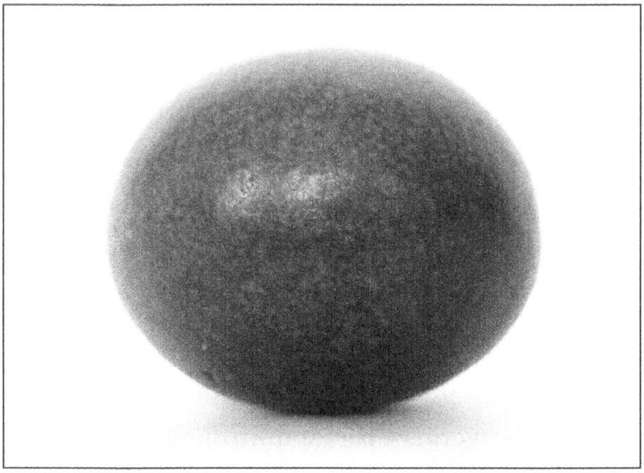

A cannon ball? A bowling ball? In fact it's a hair ball found in the stomach of a cow!

the object and facilitating access for learning. So if you can't get access to that rare bone china tea set for an object handling session by the under-fives don't despair! There are bound to be many wonderful things in your collection that are quite robust enough for the most tactile of learning events.

Of course if you don't have access to museum objects it's still quite possible to find some amazing objects to work with. Unusual objects, quirky things from charity shops, souvenirs from far distant lands, even household objects if you can present them well, will do. Junk shops, the exotic vegetables counter in your local supermarket, the

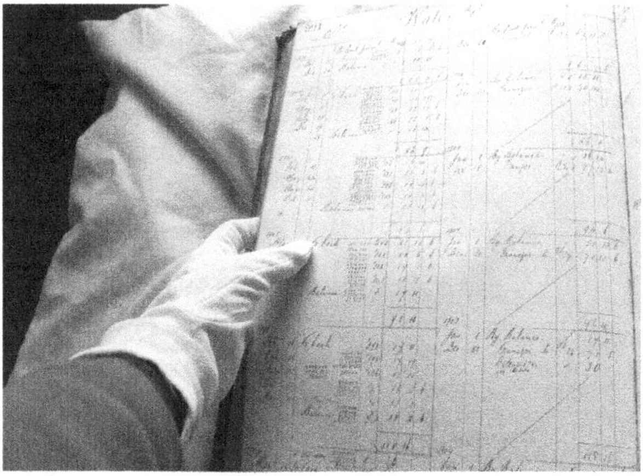

Wearing gloves to open an old book

recycling depot, fossil and mineral retailers and of course the Aladdin's cave of the internet, all contain possibilities.

Care of collections

Trying to not break the stuff you allow children (and indeed grown ups) to investigate is a major concern. Typically, the most delicate and valuable objects should not be used for the kinds of games detailed in this book. However, encouraging people to handle objects gently, even reverentially, can be a great experience. We can explain to children that the objects they are about to touch are ones that are cherished by our culture. They are objects we'd

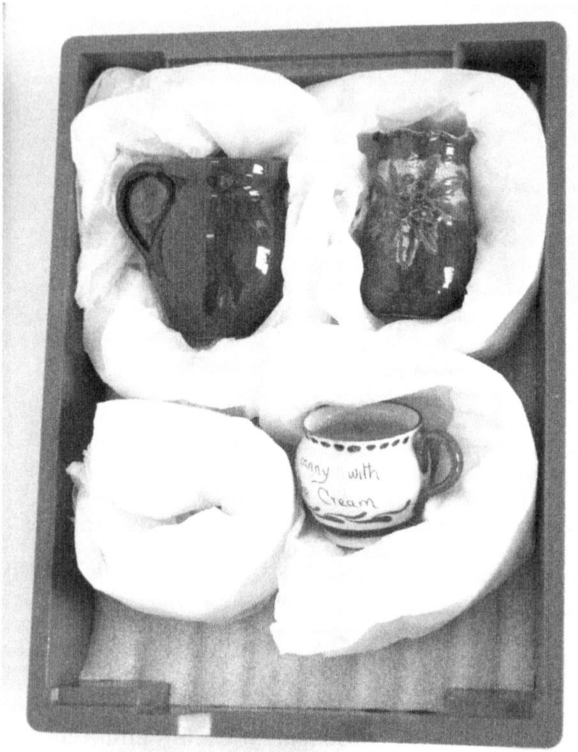

Packing objects for transport

quite like to be around in a thousand years, and so we should treat them with respect. The act of preparing the space: bubble wrap, acid-free tissue, wearing gloves and so forth, is a huge help in appreciating how we should treat these objects. Demonstrate how to handle objects safely: lifting with two hands, cradling objects rather than using handles and so on.

When transporting objects one should obviously take suitable precautions against damage. The slow unwrapping of an object, and the careful wrapping up when the session is done with, all adds to the mystique of the item and shouldn't be seen as an impediment to getting into hands-on activity.

Getting real

One of the big selling points of museum objects is that they are the real thing. Amazingly, in this age of digital data and mass production, the realness of an object is still very powerful. Sometimes the reality of an object can be obscured by first impressions. For example, looking at a cast of a dinosaur bone can be amazing, especially if it's a bone from a gigantic beast. However, children will often feel a little disappointed when told, "well

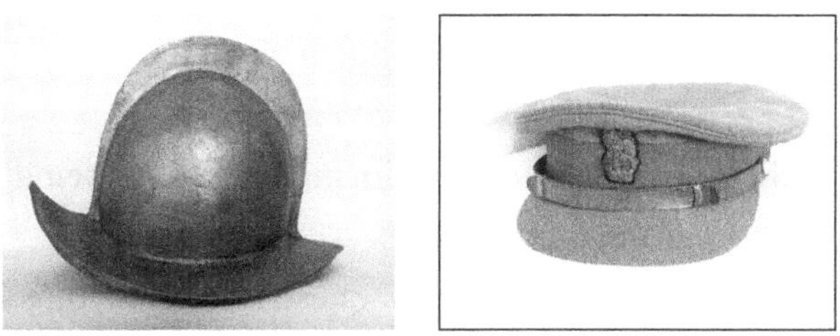

One is real, one is a replica, but which is which?

kids, this isn't the actual bone. It's an exact copy". Sometimes the quality of realness can propel a rather dull-looking thing into a new dimension. A mangled bit of metal takes on a whole different appearance when it is revealed to be genuine shrapnel from a crashed World War II aircraft.

Virtual museums, online collections, interactive exhibits and related systems can have great benefits. But there is nothing like actually handing a child a real, prehistoric hand axe (especially if you've used some of the techniques in this book to inspire a receptive frame of mind) and watching the look of amazement on their face.

Learning

There are numerous methods for describing the many aspects of the process we call learning. A typical object session might include developing historical knowledge, transferring analytical techniques, critical thinking, imaginative skills, speaking and listening and much more.

Learning, in the sense that I'm using it, includes having fun, being inspired and even being challenged or disturbed.

Try asking yourself a few questions about your sessions.

- Can you stimulate a passion for investigation in the children you're working with?
- What information will they learn?
- How will they be communicating during the session?
- How can children access what they feel about an object, and how can they express that?
- What practical skills will children acquire?
- How can they link what they already know about the world with the objects you're showing them?
- What type and range of questions emerge?
- What possibilities exist for follow-up work or exploration?

Curriculum

It is important that museums create educational sessions that link to the curriculum needs of teachers. However, probably of greater importance is creating a stimulating learning experience. Teachers are skilled in looking at an event, such as a visit to a gallery, and knowing which elements your session covered in terms of what they need to deliver. Certainly it is useful to seek advice from teachers, and to be aware of changes in policies such as the National Curriculum, but what is more important is creating a lively and inspiring event. Concentrate on delivering a rich experience and later you (or the teachers) can unpack it and see what curriculum areas have been covered. Chances are you'll be surprised how much you've achieved.

Performance

There is much to be said for considering your learning session in terms of a performance. After all, playwrights and film directors know a thing or two about how to capture and hold attention, so we are well-advised to look at their techniques. Think, for example, of the use of suspense and surprise.

If you're going to open an ancient chest and remove a bunch of interesting objects, do so slowly, carefully (this will also impress on the children that we need to handle these things with care). Cover the table before hand with acid-free tissue, bubble wrap or even a simple cloth. You may want to talk aloud to yourself: "OK, so which one shall I choose first? Ah yes, perhaps this one, yes, OK here it is...". This trick works just as well in a museum environment. You may wish to start with the objects hidden from view or covered up. Reveal them with a flourish, or perhaps ask people to close their eyes first (or even better to wear blindfolds) and focus first on what their other senses tell them if they can handle the objects before they get to see them.

It can also be fun for children to imagine what's in the box before it is even opened.

Presentation skills

As a museum professional going into a school, you have a great opportunity to provide a different style of interaction from the one the class may be familiar with. You don't have a pastoral responsibility for the children you're working with and, while it's important to have strategies for calming kids down and getting their respect and attention, you can arrive, do your stuff and leave. The benefits of this include introducing yourself in first name terms, and a reduced level of formality in the session. Try to support the teacher in the approaches they are using (for example, encourage hands to go up for questions rather than shouting out) but if you operate a different regime children are generally pretty quick to realise that some things are acceptable with one person but not with another.

Planning your session

Although it's perfectly acceptable to go along to a school with some knowledge, a bunch of objects and very little in the way of detailed planning (once you're confident in delivering a learning session on the fly) do let staff know if you need any specific resources. Each game in the later part of this book lists the resources you may need alongside it.

Make sure you have any resources to hand before the session and ideally have a couple of spares in case something goes wrong. Having a back-up plan is really helpful. In fact, it's essential if you are relying on computer equipment (although all schools have it, the quality of the equipment can vary enormously). By all means have a plan, especially if you're the kind of person who thrives on structure, but be prepared to be flexible. In the case of the games detailed in this book it's quite easy to put together a "serving suggestion" which develops a particular theme (for example moving from observation of objects, through value judgements, to hypothesis building), or concentrates on a particular aspect of learning (e.g. lots of speaking and listening games). Have a few back-up games handy that you can deploy if necessary and perhaps one game that has a very different style in case you need to change gear during the session (for example, to calm students down or rouse them from a post-lunch stupor).

Using the space

If you are running a learning session in a museum you will probably have fewer issues to consider in terms of transport of objects. In this situation the novelty of the learning space itself will have its own impact. Children will have less of an idea what to expect and will probably be more excited (which can of course have both positive and negative results).

If you are working in a school or other outreach situation it's a good idea to turn up at least fifteen minutes before the session, or a little longer if possible. This can give you a chance to move the objects into position, arrange tables, and check lighting levels (especially if you're using film or other display systems).

Have a look round the room. If you're doing a session on animals are there any relevant books on the shelves? If you're looking at bones is there a model skeleton? How about a map or globe so you can talk about other countries and point them out? How can you connect what you are exploring to things the children already have in their classroom?

Consider the physical space. If you've got a class of children, do you want to pass round objects for them to explore? If so, you may want to push those tables aside and sit in a circle on the floor (which also reduces the risk of something being dropped from a height and damaged). Alternatively, you may want to go through a set of objects, placing one or two on each table for closer work later on.

What other facilities are available? Is there a sink – ideal for demonstrating how some volcanic rocks float. Or is there a walk-in store cupboard – this can be handy for getting someone to stand in so they can't see an object when playing guessing or describing games.

You may, if time permits, want to consider how the objects are introduced into the space. Do you want a chest in the middle of the circle that children reach into? Do you want to hide objects round the room and see if the children can discover them?

Slowing down

Sometimes it's good to pause, to be still, and to prepare for an experience.

One neat technique that works brilliantly in gallery spaces, and can also be used when learning with objects away from a gallery context, is this:

- Stand or sit still, relax your body.
- Take three deep breaths, in through your nose and out through your mouth.
- With each breath reach up, as though trying to touch something on a high shelf. (If standing, try going on tip-toes.)
- As you breathe out let the shoulders droop and make a little sighing sound, restful and relaxed.
- Repeat this three times.
- Now give your body a shake; arms, legs and tilt your head from side to side. Loosen up.

Now, remember, you are an investigator, you are about to enter the gallery and see some wonderful things from a museum collection. Slow down, enter the situation as an explorer would, look around, investigate everything, talk and listen to people around you and take your time. This is a very special, magical moment...

Humans are not brains on a stick and there is much to be said for deploying a few simple relaxation techniques as part of your learning session. With younger groups of children this is expected – we let them run around to let off steam so they can concentrate better. But with older children and adults we sometimes forget that involving the body is just as important. Getting a relaxed and alert state of mind is more likely to allow wonder, curiosity and inspiration to emerge.

Working with people

Sometimes when you're presenting an object lesson you may be happy for the teachers to take a back seat. But don't be afraid to ask for their help if you want it. One useful technique is to ask the teacher to put up their hand if you use a word they think needs more explaining. This can also work well if you're delivering a session with another professional. For example, I once provided a session for some secondary school children which involved a professional archaeologist. More used to lecturing to post-graduate students, he would say things like, "after the last glacial there were all kinds of mega flora and fauna in the British Isles". My job was to put my hand up and say, "Sorry, do you mean ice-age – and mega what?" I was asking the questions that perhaps many of the students would have liked to ask but probably felt too self-conscious to.

There will probably be plenty of situations where you might need a volunteer from the class. To try on the replica Roman military helmet, for example, or test how heavy a sample of iron ore is. Using a single person in this way, asking their name, and thanking them afterwards, can be useful if you have time pressures that mean not everyone is going to get to dress-up or handle a specimen.

Don't be afraid to listen to other opinions. It's very easy when we are placed in the role of expert to become defensive about what we know (or think we know). You may find yourself presenting an object in the company of someone who knows more, or who has noticed something about it you simply hadn't. Include this information in your presentation and games. An essential point here is to make children aware that we are all, all the time, figuring things out. None of us have a monopoly of knowledge and it's worth framing what you do understand in terms of "what I've read/experienced/seen", this makes knowledge into a shared experience rather than a possession. The aim of all the games detailed here is to present learning, and even knowledge, as something we *do* (rather than *have*). New experiences (including information from others) help develop and expand our knowledge. What we know, we should hold lightly. If you present a prehistoric flint as an arrow head, and some bright spark claims that it's more likely to be a scraper, then you have a choice either to feel this as a possibility for learning more about the world (even if it is only to understand why the other person thinks you're wrong), or to feel challenged, even attacked.

By acknowledging that learning is a fluid, on-going process we remain more flexible, better able to learn new things and less likely to fall prey to dogmatism. If we can convey this to young people then we are encouraging them to be curious, to think for themselves, to question authority, and to make judgements about the relative worth of different sources of information. These are essential abilities for successful life-long learners.

Story

It is possible to use to embed your session within a story. This generally works best either with younger children (where, for example, a puppet could be the investigator which gets to discover various objects or rooms in the museum) or when the children have seen the story a couple of times. The Think Tank method, developed by Barnstaple Museum is a good example of this. A film is used to tell the story of an alien who abducts objects from a museum collection. The objects then appear in the classroom for our *galacternauts* (i.e. the children) to investigate (see the final section of this book for more details). For those classes who have seen the film more than once the narrative sets up an expectation of excitement and curiosity.

Be a little cautious in developing too elaborate a story. The fascination of the objects themselves, and your cunning ways for getting the children to engage with them, may well be sufficient.

Dressing up is a slightly different method of using a story and there are some fantastic possibilities that may emerge if you choose to don doublet and hose or a military uniform. In-character sessions can be effective but work best if you've primed the teacher beforehand to ask some particular questions or otherwise get the discussion going. Remember, you may think you look great but to some children you will look just weird or perhaps threatening. This approach usually works best in an appropriate (historic) setting rather than in a classroom.

Historical clothing can be worn just by you when presenting the session or by one or more members of the class. Costumes need not be elaborate, especially when working with junior school children: hats, shawls and tabards will often suffice. If you need to make a transition between one role (top-hatted and formally-dressed Victorian gentleman) and another (museum learning officer) it's a good idea to have some formal process to make this transition. Asking the children to shout a magic word, or disappearing into that store cupboard and re-appearing in your new guise are helpful. This eases the imaginative transition between roles for your audience and is the presentational equivalent of punctuation in writing (or flash powder in a pantomime).

If you're going to present the investigation of objects as a scientific endeavour you could try wearing a white lab coat. If possible all the children could dress up in this way. Wearing white gloves will allow them to enter an analytical role and will help impress on them the need to handle objects carefully. Adopting a scientific frame of reference can also turn a familiar object into an unfamiliar one. A potato, for instance, can appear quite different if we are wearing an apron and cutting it up into chips or wearing protective goggles, slicing it with a scalpel and looking at it under a microscope.

Magnifying glasses are perhaps the most useful tools you can have with you when delivering a

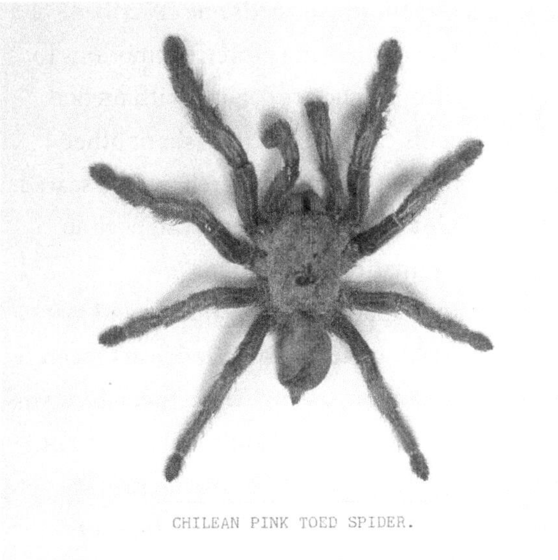

It's a scary specimen!

learning session. Not only do they allow us to look closely at objects but they signify investigation, close observation and examination. As with all objects, a magnifying glass carries both a literal function and an imaginative or cultural meaning.

Experiences

Working with objects can invoke all kinds of experiences. People who are suffering from bereavement, for instance, may find working with animal remains tremendously unsettling.

Games, such as the grave goods one described later in the book, can bring powerful emotions to the surface. People who are dealing with mental health problems can find dolls, masks or other objects frightening. Young children may be scared of stuffed animals and adolescents can have an unnerving fascination for weapons.

All of these experiences are valuable and just because something is difficult that doesn't mean that it isn't "good" or "useful". Objects can bring us face-to-face with our fears. While it is important that the people leading the session can manage a difficult situation successfully, outbursts of emotion and even upsetting experiences can be an important part of learning, they don't represent a failure.

The vast majority of sessions will focus on creativity, curiosity, discovery and imagination but fear, trouble and sadness are also feelings that can emerge. Be prepared for these. One of the most important elements in these situations is to make the person who is experiencing difficult feelings appreciate that they are not alone. If a child finds grief welling up when they see an object that is somehow associated with a recently deceased family member, make sure they know their feelings are not unique. This is not the same as asking them to "buck up and get over it". Rather it is about acknowledging our shared human condition. Those of us who have not experienced grief will inevitably do so at some stage in our lives. Those who are experiencing it now need to know they have the understanding of those who share their feelings and the respect of those who have yet to feel that way.

It's wise to have at least one other adult available who can be there to support anyone who encounters difficult feelings in a session. Often the person who is upset will need to leave the room in which the offending object is located and have some time out. If possible it's helpful if they can come back into the room later in the session, either when the object is packed away or the game completed or, if they feel they can manage it, before that.

Whether they choose to return to the session or not, it is valuable for the child to talk about their emotions. It's also a good idea to have the museum educator meet the child again after the session so that the child can express their feelings. Such a meeting (which need not be more elaborate than a "Hello again Stanley, are you feeling a bit better now?") also helps the child understand that it was their own feelings evoked by the object that have come up and not directly the fault of anyone else. Solidarity can also be shared in this situation. In one session I spoke openly to a group of children about how the skull of a young Saxon child was a powerful and disturbing object for me (I'd just become a father). Recognising that these outbursts of feeling are a normal part of human experience is essential.

Games

The following are games that you can play with objects. Most of the games given here will work for any object or collections of objects. However I've also included a few that are object-specific – for example, games which require an object that can be seen through (such as a porthole or telescope), and games which require bones (or tusks, or horns). I've deliberately not included details of age ranges, or skills that are being developed by each game. The reason for this is that the majority of games can be adapted for use with different abilities and ages. If in doubt, simply spend a little time imagining your group playing the game. Think through the steps, the objects and the personalities involved. If you don't know the group, try to imagine the game with the age and ability range you're working with.

By doing so you can see how the game might need amending to suit the players, and you may be able to head off potential problems before you run the session for real.

The majority of games will support language skills. Even those games which are focused around drawing or drama will generate talk. Try to leave time for this process. Although it can be fun to create a sense of urgency in your activities (the Think Tank system does this by presenting the idea that the abducted museum objects only have one hour to be examined before they are teleported back) don't try to cram too many activities into a session. Allow time for talking, asking questions, considering ideas and so on.

One piece of additional information I have included with each game is an indication of what resources you may need. Some games call for photographs of the objects you are exploring; others will need you to have a stop watch or pencil and paper. For many of these activities, magnifying glasses will help children look in greater detail at the objects, and will help slow them down so they can pay more attention. For drama-based games you'll need sufficient space to break into smaller groups and then to perform.

The games presented here are deliberately not arranged thematically! This is to encourage you to dip into this book, and see which techniques catch your eye. Leaf through the games, see which ones would blend together and be suitable for the group or objects you're using. See which games can be merged together to create new versions – and of course create your own! There are several blank pages at the back of the book where you can add your own games and make notes. Each game has some space beneath it where you can make observations and comments. Think of this book as a working manual rather than textbook.

GAMES

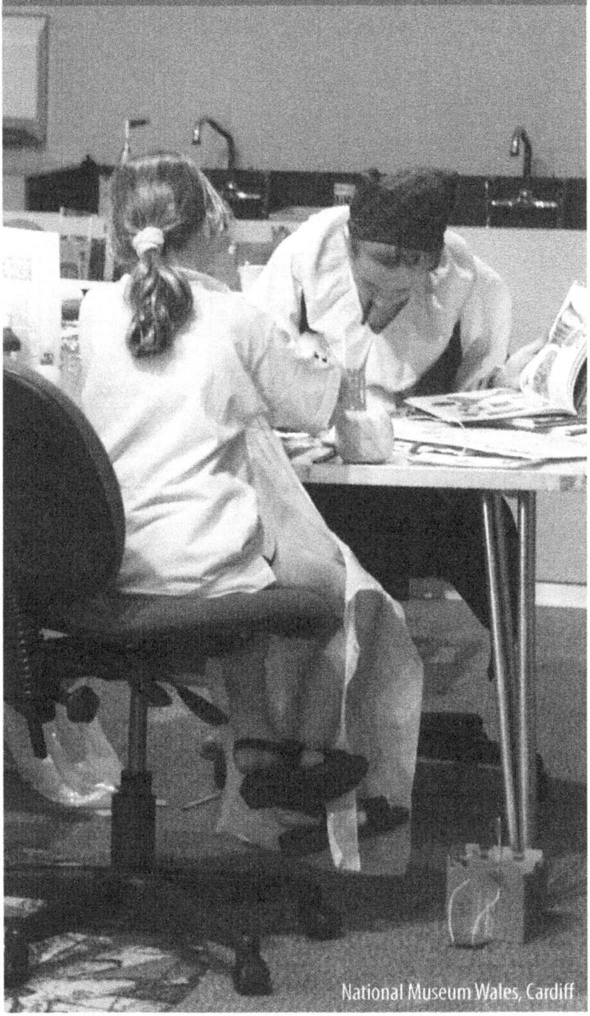

National Museum Wales, Cardiff

1

Find A Family

Resources: if the objects are too delicate to handle, or the group is large, cards with pictures of the objects on. Hoops, ropes or some other method to create circles.

Ideally this game can be played in small groups. Arrange your objects into sets or families.

You may wish to introduce the idea of the sets intersecting, with circles linked together and objects that have a foot in both camps in the middle. Perhaps some objects need to lie outside of the families?

Spread all the cards/objects out so everyone in the group can see what they are working with and let the discussions unfold. This game provides a good opportunity to practice consensus decision making.

After the objects are arranged ask one child, as the spokesperson for the group, to explain why they made the choices they did. Move round each group listening to the different strategies that have been used. Encourage each group to listen to the others; are the strategies that other groups used very different?

You may wish to summarise the different approaches to this problem. One group may have gone for a method which is more like that of the conservator – i.e. what is the object made from; others may have a more thematic approach. The division of objects into natural/cultural is a very common answer to this task, and can be a great springboard into exploring what these classifications mean to us.

2

Guess What!

Resources required: none.

One person selects an object from the collection. Without revealing their choice, they then describe it in detail to the others who visualise it (ideally with their eyes closed) and then either draw it and/or guess at its identity.

As a slight variation of this game you might choose to use a set range of questions which the person doing the describing must answer, for example:

- How big is it?
- How does it feel? (e.g. rough or smooth, heavy or light, sturdy or delicate)
- What colour is it?
- What is its shape?
- Are there any patterns or writing on it?

Once the identity of the object has been guessed another person can have a go at describing.

A time element can be useful and fun when playing this game. You might, for example, give the speaker a limit of 30 seconds to describe the object and limit the guesses or drawing time for the object to 60 seconds.

3

Translations In Time

Resources: none.

A simple little exercise in imagination but one that can be lots of fun. This is best played with a range of older household items. Children are asked to translate an object into its modern equivalent. For example:

Coins = credit card
Typewriter = computer
Flat iron = electric iron
Glass bottle = plastic bottle
Quill = Biro

You might award points for particularly cunning answers. For example a flat iron could be translated into crease-proof fabric, or a quill into a computer keyboard.

4

Time Teams

Resources required: a range of objects or, if the objects are too delicate, cards with pictures of the objects on.

Developing a chronology can be a challenging task for young children but is certainly an important one. This game can lead into discussions not only of how old different objects are but also of what evidence we use to estimate their age.

Place the objects themselves, or cards with pictures of the objects on, into chronological order. This game works best in small groups and helps build negotiation skills but can equally be adapted by using class voting as a way of deciding which object is placed where.

Find out why the objects were placed in the order that they were. Was it because some things looked shiny that people thought they were newer? Was it because some objects were not recognised that they were imagined as being older? Are there replica or "fake" objects in the collection that might confuse the timeline? Are some objects shaped similarly to the ones we use now but were in fact made hundreds of years ago?

This game can be a good time to reveal some factual information about your objects. Arrange them into the right order and explain why you are placing them where you do. Talk about how some objects, such as a lion skull, are hard to date and could be ten or 1000 years old.

Remember a timeline might also have objects of roughly the same age. There may also be objects where we simply don't know where they fit.

5

Artyfacts

Resources required: drawing paper and pencils/crayons/pens etc.

Look closely at the objects in your collection. If possible handle them, look at them through magnifying glasses and get to know them.

Now try drawing one or more objects. Keep in mind the following possibilities:

- The use of shading to show the structure of the object or other features.
- Perhaps choosing different techniques (e.g. charcoal vs. technical drawing pen) depending on the form of the object.
- Counting and reading – does your drawing show the right number of spouts/hooks/holes etc. Have you reproduced the markings, inscriptions or label on it accurately?

Show the drawings to the person next to you. Can they tell what you've drawn?

Drawing is one of the most common activities children are asked to do with museum objects. They will benefit if you are able to draw as well and perhaps share some basic techniques with them (e.g. using different pressures to change a pencil line, light sketching, drawing an ellipse, measuring using the pencil with one eye closed).

Encourage children who say they can't draw to find a style that works for them – for some this might be a technical-style diagram. For others a cartoon style. Ask them to draw what they see (at least in this game) but allow them to experiment with different styles until they relax and begin to have fun.

You can make this a fast-paced exercise but it can also be done very slowly and thoughtfully (if you're treating this game more like a "proper" art lesson why not try some music in the background to help the artists relax?)

6

Practical Joker

Resources required: none.

Dream up a wicked practical joke using one or more of the objects in the collection. Examples include such wizard wheezes as:

- Placing a crocodile head in your sister's bed.
- Asking your brother to watch the stuffed hawk very hard because it's about to move.
- Telling your dad that you had just dug up the Roman coin in the back garden.
- Explaining to mum that the Victorian glove stretcher was what ladies used to remove unsightly nasal hairs and she should give it a go...

Mime Time

Resources required: sufficient space to do drama work.

One person picks an object and does not reveal their choice. They then mime the object and their classmates guess which one it is. The mime could relate to the form, the use of the object, or perhaps some other aspect of it (such as its manufacture or discovery).

This is a great game for engaging children who may not be strong with spoken language. It is also a potential confidence builder for quieter kids.

You could informally award points not just to guesses but also to people who do particularly clever or beautiful mimes. In this way you are rewarding the process as well as the result.

8

Get the Picture

Resources required: none.

This can be done in pairs or as a whole class.

Choose an object in your mind. Close your eyes and imagine the scene when it was new. What is under it, behind it, next to it, around it? Are there any sounds or smells in this scene? Now describe the scene to your partner or group and see if they can guess which object you are thinking about.

9

That's My Object!

Resources required: drawing materials.

This game works well in pairs.

Describe or draw the person who used or owned the object when it was new. (This could lead to a discussion of gender roles then and now.) Talk with your partner about who you think owned a particular object. Ask yourselves: How old were they? Were they male or female? Were they rich or poor? What were they wearing? Where would you have found this person living or working? What else could you guess about the owner?

Find a new partner and describe your person to them. Can they guess which object you imagine they are connected to?

10

Just a Minute

Resources required: stop watch.

You need two teams to play this game. A person from one team describes one of the objects without hesitation, deviation or repetition. If they do hesitate or repeat themselves, anyone from the opposing team can interrupt by putting up their hand, and challenge them. If the interrupter is correct, they take over for the rest of the minute and if they make it to the end of the minute, their team gets a point.

This is a great language game which generally works best with slightly older children. It's a good plan to put the teacher in the role of timekeeper and to decide any disputes!

11

Twenty Questions

Resources required: none.

One child chooses, without indicating their choice, an object from the collection. The class then aims to guess the identity of the object in only 20 questions. Each question needs to have a *yes* or *no* answer.

You might want to suggest some questions that will get good results, for example:

- Is it ....?
- Does it....?
- Can you... with it?

Once the 20 questions are asked the class can make a guess as to the identity of the mystery object. Depending on the skill level of the group there are lots of subtle variations of the rules to explore. What happens if you have two teams, each just gets ten questions and a wrong guess by one team means that a point is automatically given to their opponents (or perhaps they lose the right to ask any more questions)? What is the smallest number of questions that can be used to guess the identity of an object? Perhaps the points for a correct answer decrease the more questions are asked?

Since the basic premise of the game is very simple and the rules so flexible, this game can be a good way of getting learners to appreciate the game process, rule making and breaking, and come up with their own versions of the activity.

12

Freeze Frame

Resources required: some space.

In a small group secretly select one of the objects. Now create a freeze frame of people in the "picture" around the object at the time it was discovered or in use.

Can you create a motionless tableau so that other members of the class can guess the object you've chosen?

13

The Name Game

Resources required: labels (eg Post-it notes), pens.

Depending on the age and ability range of the group there are a number of different variations of this game.

Naming labels are created and handed out or the teacher reads out the names of the objects and the children write them down, a good opportunity to practice spelling.

The labels are then placed by the children beside the appropriate object. This game also provides a good opportunity for the teacher to explain how we can feel nervous if our opinion conflicts with the majority verdict. Having a couple of unusual objects, or ones that are very likely to be misidentified, can help make this point

14

Labelling

Resources required: writing materials, labels (old style luggage labels are great for this).

Lots of museum objects are labelled but why do the labels look the way they do? What are all those mysterious numbers about? This game is a good opportunity to explain the accessioning process and labelling. Using the objects you provide, make labels for each one. Some labels could be of the kind that you see in museums; perhaps with code numbers (children might invent their own coding system). Labels could also be made with descriptions of each object on them and perhaps one or more key facts. Labels like these often sit alongside objects in a museum so what information should they contain?

Now look at the labels in the room where the group are working. Check out labels on clothes, near fire exits, look at how many there are! You could try to make labels in the modern style for objects from the museum collection: *World War II bayonet – danger! Sharp! Do not stick into body.*

15

Riddle in the Middle

Resources required: writing materials.

Riddles can be created individually or in groups. These could be descriptive riddles such as:

A circle of brass
Around my open eye
Glassy and strong
Across the sea I spy
What am I?
(Answer: a port hole)

Iron roof, glass walls
Burns and burns, but never falls
What am I?
(Answer: a lantern)

More complex riddles can use combinations of words to indicate the letters that go to make up the answer, for instance:

My first is in ocean but never in sea,
My second's in wasp but never in bee,
My third is in glider and also in flight,
My whole is a creature that comes out at night.
What am I?
(Answer: an owl)

16

History Mysteries

Resources required: writing materials.

In groups, choose an object and think about the questions that begin:

Who?
When?
What?
Where?
How?
Why?

Create a story using what you have learned about the object so far. Start with a setting (place and time). Continue the story up until today.

How believable are your stories? Which are the most interesting or exciting?

A variation of this game: in groups, choose an object and sit in a circle. Elect a person to start the story of the life of the object from its first appearance in the world. Go back in time as far as you want, for example, to the acorn that fell to the ground and became the tree that provided the wood from which the object was made.

Take turns going round the circle to tell the next stage of the story, based on what you have already learned or guessed about the object. The person speaking decides when to stop talking. Perhaps the stages of the story will become obvious or perhaps narrators should have 30 seconds each?

If someone veers off in a direction you were not expecting still try to carry on from where they left off. Part of the skill of the storyteller is to make connections and go where the story takes you. If you can't think of anything to say, you can pass and maybe have a go next time round.

17

Commercial Break

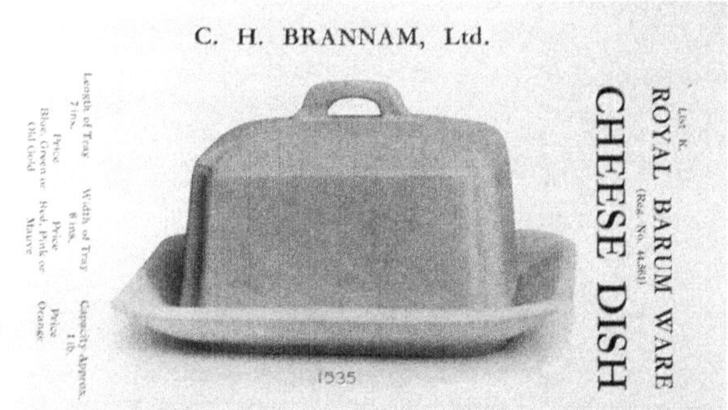

How would this product be advertised today?

Resources required: none (although some space for drama work will be useful).

Using guess work, prior knowledge and imagination decide what an unusual object may have been used for and create a 30-second advert for it. The advertisement could be imagined as a television commercial or, in keeping with the time the object was created, it could be an advert in the form of the patter of a travelling salesman.

What would make you want to buy your object? How would it improve your everyday life? If you are not sure what it is for – make it your invention and you decide what it is and what it does. Sell it to your classmates. After a few people have had a go, have a vote or discussion as to which item members of the class would actually spend their money on.

This activity lends itself to follow-up work. How were things in the past advertised? How did people advertise before film, TV, the internet? Look at and design advertising for your object. How does the advert feel if you use ultra-modern design versus retro styles to market your product?

18

The Balloon Debate

Resources required: none.

A classic game which can deal with some very real issues (such as the problems of disposal in museums).

Imagine that you are in a balloon or a crashing spacecraft. Some of the objects are going to need to be jettisoned in order to reduce the weight and save the crew.

This game often works best by selecting a chairperson to run the meeting. The chair suggests an object to throw out and the rest of the group raise their hands to argue for or against the chair's selection. In all cases a reason needs to be given for disposing or keeping and object (though of course reasons can be highly emotive).

Votes are cast once the arguments are made and the object is either kept or chucked out. If the class is unwilling to throw anything out you might want to press them by alluding to the very real peril the balloon is in. Hard decisions will have to be made!

19

What Next?

Resources: writing materials, large sheets of paper, marker pens and maybe cameras.

A useful exercise before the objects are packed away this one. Make a list of all the questions that still haven't been answered in the session. You may want to place some of the objects (or write their names) in the centre of a large sheet of paper and create a mind-map or spider diagram of questions, remarks and thoughts.

Take photographs of the objects. Especially any features that were not fully explained.

Make a list of spin-off questions that have emerged from discussions. These may not be directly related to the objects but are still important to follow up. In this way the teacher can capture all those questions, remarks and observations that perhaps were kept to one side in order to keep the class on task. Try to follow these questions up as soon as practical after the session while the memory of the objects is still fresh.

20

Discovery Diary

Resources: writing materials.

Choose one object and write a short diary extract, fictional story, newspaper article or script about it. You may wish to start by giving children the first line of the story. Perhaps including some real or imagined historical data, for instance:

> *Charles Darwin's Diary, 2 October 1836. Today we are landing at Falmouth and I have as part of the collection I am bringing back to England the most remarkable specimen...*
>
> Or:
>
> *Enemy bombing ends with great loss of life. At 03:00 hours this morning the Luftwaffe launched two major raids over the North East of England. The shattered wreckage of enemy aircraft was left...*

Diary extracts could focus on the discovery, invention or capture of the object. Take the writing a step further by styling the text to resemble a real diary entry; perhaps written using a dipping ink pen, a typed letter, a tea-stained "parchment" or even a coded message.

21

Speaking as the Object

Resources required: none – though writing materials may come in handy.

There are lots of variations of this game, some of which could involve creative writing, poetry or prose of the type suggested in the previous *Diary Extracts* game). The basic idea is to give the object a voice. If it could speak what would it say?

The process that works for most people is to begin by talking about the object, then gradually move "inwards" until they can imagine the world from the perspective of the object itself.

For example you could try a session structured in the following way:

- Begin by revealing the objects, allow them to be handled. Ask children to write lists or make spider diagrams of ideas, impressions, and observations about each object.
- Tell the children a bit about each object, get them to ask questions and make deductions about the objects.
- Ask one person to describe the object in detail to another person.
- Ask them to write as though they were the object itself.

This process can form the basic frame for a session, moving from observation, providing information, describing and finally identifying with the object.

When speaking as the object you might want children to write or perform. What type of voice would a 1800s man-trap have? What style of talk would you expect from an Ancient Egyptian object? What happens when you mix styles, could a spinning wheel produce a rap? Could a pair of scales from a rural market talk like a royal personage?

Speaking as the object, especially if it has been approached by gradually getting people in the right frame of mind, can be a powerful activity. This is one of the approaches to working with objects that can have tremendous therapeutic benefits. In short, people will speak "about" the object or "for" the object but are, of course, often really speaking about themselves. These feelings are not located in the object but in our relationship to it. For example, seeing a *manilla* (the metal tokens used to trade in slaves from West Africa) you could see embodied in such an object the story of human triumph against adversity. The brave story of people sold into bondage and the long road to liberation exemplified by individuals such as Rosa Parks and Martin Luther King. However, you could equally see the object as emblematic of human brutality, or the continued forms of economic and prison slavery that exist today. How we see things inevitably says as much about us as it does about the things themselves.

Another possible dimension to this kind of activity is to record what is being said. This could involve recording a poem that has been written from the point of view of an object, or it may involve recording the conversation that unfolds in a more informal way. How does it feel to listen back to how children made the object speak after a week, six weeks, longer?

22

Connected Tales

Resources required: none.

Pick three objects (or more) and come up with a story that links them together. These stories can be spoken or written in some form.

Try telling the story to an audience but missing out the name of the objects themselves. Is it obvious which objects the story is about?

You can also try placing the objects on the floor, or on a large sheet of paper, and drawing lines between them as you make your connections. The lines can be labelled with keywords then the next person can draw theirs in a different colour. This can eventually create a huge, complex spider diagram or mind-map.

23

Crossword Clues

Resources required: writing materials.

Create a simple crossword with associated clues for some or all of the objects in the collection.

There are various handy bits of software on the internet that can help in the creation of crossword grids. Explore the difference between simple and more complex, cryptic clues.

24

Anagram

Resources required: writing materials.

Try taking the name of each object and see if you can make an anagram of it. Try scrambling two words together. Create some of these and try them out on other members of the class. Can they figure out the anagram?

There are free programs available on the internet that will create anagrams for you. These might be useful if you'd like to set a task of unscrambling some anagrams rather than creating them. This can also be interesting where one or more of the encrypted words are now uncommon – eg fire dog, terret ring, adze.

25

Size Matters

Resources: tape measure or other measuring devices can be handy for this game.

There are lots of variations of this game. The basic format is to ask the children to study the objects (picking them up if this is possible) and then return them to the tables. Children now estimate the dimensions of some of the objects. If you want to create a competitive environment you can award points for the person or team who gets closest to the actual measurement. You may also want to see what differences emerge if estimates are made before and then after handling.

With a little preparation it can also be informative to compare the objects in the collection with ancient or modern, bigger or smaller versions. Look at a Victorian woman's shoe: what was the average height in Victorian England, what is it now? An elephant tusk may be big but how much larger was a mammoth tusk?

26

X Marks The Spot

Resources: pre-printed maps, large sheets of paper, drawing equipment and access to the Internet might help.

Ask the children to select one or more objects from the collection. Their task is then to create or find a map which locates their chosen object. They could drawing a fictional map or research a real one.

27

Make Me An Object!

Resources: modelling clay, play dough or similar.

We often ask children to observe and then draw objects but sometimes it's more satisfying to make them. This can be done with any resources available, from junk modelling or play dough, to clay intended to be fired. Objects such as flint hand axes, fossils and geological samples are particularly good to make in 3D.

Close Up

Resources: drawing materials and magnifying glasses can help.

Draw or photograph a detail of one or more objects. This could be as small as a single nail or taken from an unusual angle such as the base of old bottle. Pictures can then be hung on the walls, or shown on a computer and children can try to guess which detail comes from which object.

This game is a great way to get children to slow down and to observe closely.

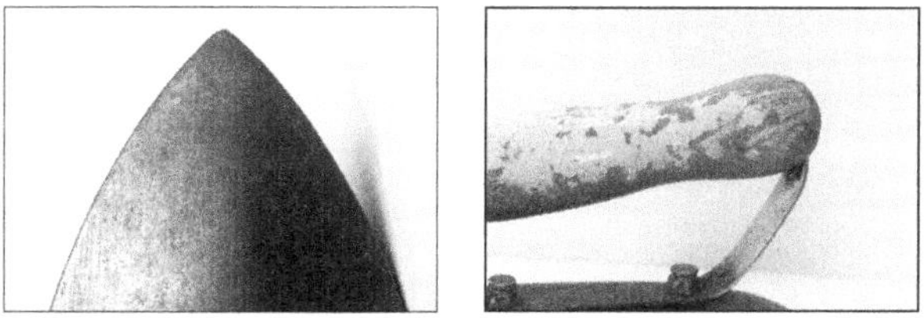

Parts of an early electric iron photographed from an odd angle

29

Info Centre

Resources: a space to put up information near where the collection is situated.

Simply make a space near the collection if you've got use of it for several days. Ideas, information, questions, pictures of similar objects, diagrams and more information can then be posted on the wall creating a resource that grows over time.

30

Vital Statistics

Resources: lots of measuring equipment such as scales, tape measures, graph paper etc.

How many vital statistics is it possible to draw out from the object? Can you find its weight, height, volume? What analysis can't be conducted because the object is too delicate or valuable? What things could you find out if it was possible to use destructive investigation techniques? Try these out on objects that are suitable. How do we balance our desire to know (e.g. what is inside a fossil) with the fact that by cutting it we are changing and perhaps destroying it forever?

Tables and graphs can be created of the data that gets discovered. Counting can also help inform drawing or modelling practices.

31

Letter Rack

Resources required: writing materials.

Children write a letter to one of their classmates (or someone else) suggesting that they visit the museum in order to see the amazing objects. In the letter they describe the object(s) and perhaps suggest how the person they are writing to may feel when they see it.

It can be fun to try writing your letter on tea-stained paper. You can also try ripping the edges and even burning the paper to get that authentic ancient parchment look. Try exploring other ways of writing: italic letters, copper plate, brushes, quills even hieroglyphics or World War II codes and ciphers.

Don't forget to really post them if writing to classmates!

32

Filling In The Fragments

Resources required: drawing materials.

Pottery can make for some interesting reconstruction processes. From the curve of a section it is usually possible to work out the circumference of the original vessel. The slope of the fragment can also suggest how deep the vessel was. Try making reconstructions of the original design. This game will work for many types of object. Consider what things we may not be able to know: the colours of fossilised animals, the presence of wood in the long-vanished handle of a stone tool.

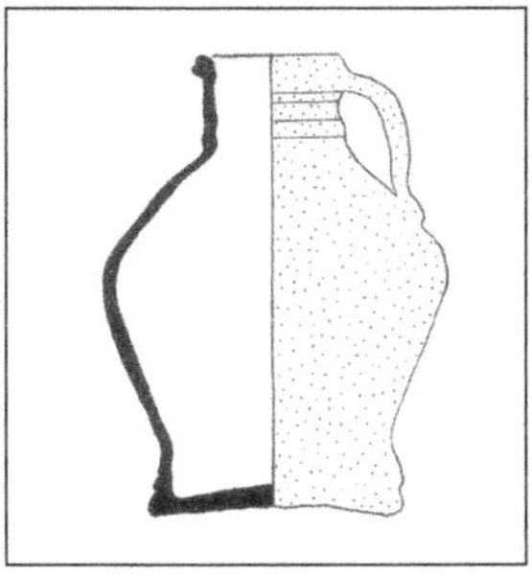

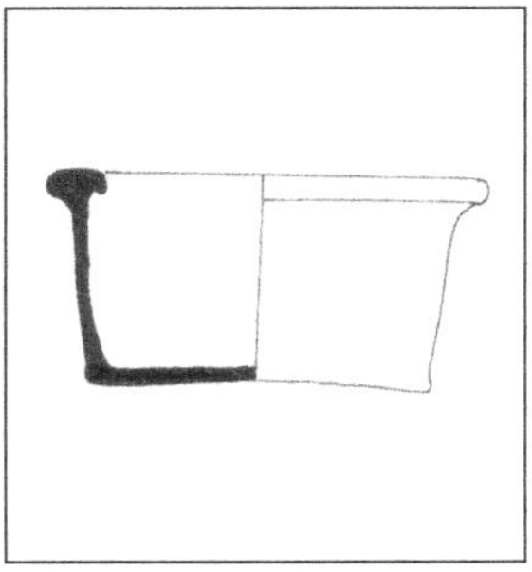

From just a small pottery fragment we can start to guess what the original shape may have been

33

Call My Bluff

Resources: prepared true and bluff cards.

Three people offer plausible explanations for each object. Obviously this works especially well with obscure objects. However, even with known objects this game can still be played. The choices could be between real or false definitions, or between several tales relating to the object.

Is it a replica or the real thing? Each person could give a plausible story of how the object was discovered or perhaps how it was made in factory only weeks ago?

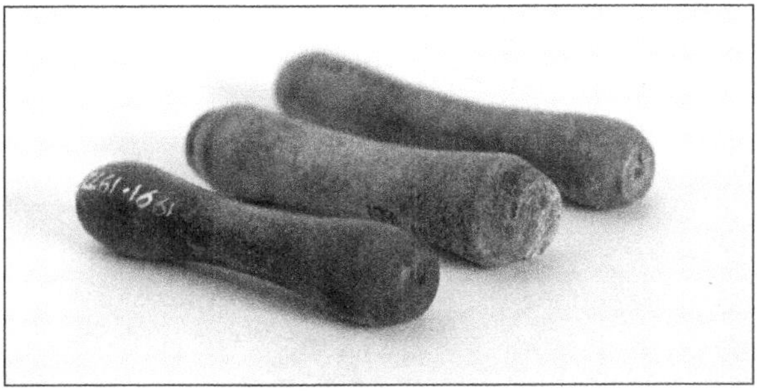

So what are these mysterious objects?

34

Values and Status

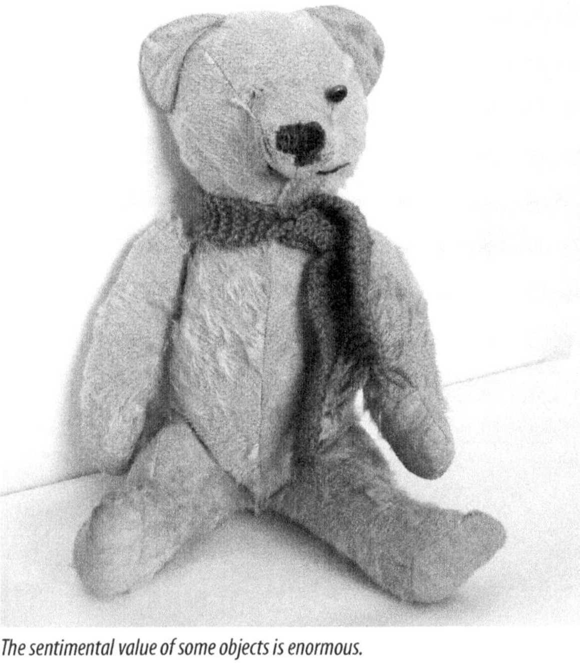

The sentimental value of some objects is enormous.

Resources required: writing materials and perhaps hoops for grouping objects into families.

This is a game that can develop in a number of ways. Using the objects themselves, cards with pictures of each object, or pieces of paper with drawings/words on, group the objects together. Place all the "high status" objects in one group. This could mean objects that are financially valuable, objects used or valued by members of the ruling groups in a culture, or perhaps objects that are likely to have great (sentimental) value. Group the other objects into middle and low status or value groups. This can be done as an exercise in smaller groups and can lead to some excellent discussions about the different ideas of value and importance attached to the things around us.

35

Back to the Future

Resources required: whatever is in your immediate environment.

Make a collection of objects from around the room the group are in now. Which objects would be easy to interpret in, say, 100 years time and which would be more difficult? What connections exist between the objects in the museum collection and the objects you've found in the room? Which objects maintain the same basic forms over time, such as clothes pegs or shoes? What are the differences in materials, markings?

What differences exist in terms of how easily objects can be repaired, re-charged or re-used (contrast for example a dipping ink pen with a non-refillable biro). What will happen to the object after it is beyond repair (contrast the fact that leather shoes can be composted whereas plastic ones might exist for thousands of years). Look at objects that are around today which are falling out of use (an audio cassette, vinyl record, a 3.5 inch floppy disk): how long until no-one knows what they are?

36

Feely Bags

Resources required: cloth bag or similar and drawing equipment.

Place a suitable object in a cloth bag, or a box with a hole cut in the side, reach in and feel the object. Ask the children to describe or draw what they feel. This delightfully simple game can be the springboard for conversations about perception, how we make sense of the world and risk-taking.

The drawings could be literal and realistic ("I could feel it was a flat iron") or abstract ("I've drawn the feelings of cold, smooth and heavy").

37

Kim's Game Variations

Resources required: a cloth to cover the objects.

Ask the group to look at the objects in the collection. Give them at least two minutes. Then cover the objects with a cloth. Kim's Game simply requires the children to see how many of the objects they can recall (perhaps writing or calling out answers). A variation of this is to ask children to draw the objects as accurately as they can from memory. Another variation of this game is to ask about different aspects of the objects in the collection – how many things were made of wood? How many things made of clay? How many military-looking objects?

If you know any memory techniques (such as using visualisation skills) you could try teaching these and seeing if that helps the children's recall.

38

Giant Drawing

Resources required: drawing materials.

Another a drawing exercise but one that relies on having a bit of space. A big sheet of paper, such as a roll of lining paper, can be used. Draw one or more of the objects – big! Experiment with providing different media for the drawing such as charcoal, chalks (great outdoors on the pavement) or wax crayons.

39

Martian Game

Resources required: a voice recorder can add an extra element to this game.

A game to play in pairs or small groups. One person pretends to be an alien (it might be useful for them to spend some time imagining their world and in what ways it differs from Earth) and asks questions about one of the human objects. The other person attempts to interpret and explain the object. These conversations can be great fun and, if participants are not too embarrassed, are often worthwhile recording and playing back so that the wider group can hear what went on.

40

A Case of Mystery

Resources required: a suitable container for your objects.

Prepare a collection of objects and suggest that they have been found together in an item of luggage left at a station or on a boat. (It's even better if you can present the objects in a mysterious-looking box, treasure chest, or hi-tech flight case). Ask children to come up with a tale that explains how and why these objects came to be in the lost case.

You can try this exercise with several groups: you'll probably find that presenting the collection in a silver flight case generates very different stories compared to objects that are "found" in an old packing crate.

41

Grave Goods

Resources required: none.

Ask one person to lie down or mark out an outline of a body on the floor. Members of the class take turns to add grave goods by the side of (or even on) the "corpse". Depending on the delicacy of the object either it or a picture card of the object are placed. As each object is added, the person doing so has to explain how the object represents the person's life, or will in some way be needed in the afterlife:

- "I am adding these shoes for our dear departed friend so she can walk easily through Heaven's gate."
- "Let this shell rest with our dear departed friend to remind her always of the sea she loved."
- "By placing this sword by his side I ensure that this warrior shall find his place in Valhalla!"

This exercise works really well to help children make sense of cultures such as the Ancient Egyptians who provided elaborate grave goods. Once all the objects are placed around the "body" an interesting discussion can be started: what would be left after, say, 500 years in the earth? What materials would have rotted and which would remain relatively unchanged? Could an archaeologist excavating the site guess the reasons why the grave goods were added?

42

Cultures of Meaning

Resources required: images of people from different cultures can help.

When we meet an object, we inevitably bring our own experiences, prejudices and cultures with us as we interact with items in a collection. Ask children to imagine themselves as being from different cultures. How might they think differently about each object if they were a Native American, an Inuit, a person from the 25th century, a devout Christian from medieval Europe? To give an example of how different our perceptions can be, try to find some clear examples: the swastika as the insignia of the Nazi party versus the swastika as a symbol of life in Hindu religion is a clear instance of this process.

You may wish to create a series of masks or small cut-out figures representing different cultures and periods of history. These can be used by the children to engage with the objects as though from the perspective of the masks or figures used.

43

Makers' Marks

Resources required: drawing and writing materials.

Ask children to explain to each other, or to the group, how they think each object was manufactured. Diagrams or storyboards can be drawn showing the main processes. Points can be awarded for the most accurate or funniest accounts of how each object came to be. Look closely at each object: are there examples of makers' marks, stamps, or even thumb-prints in clay?

44

Rapid-Fire Research

Resources required: writing materials, a library, and one or more Internet connections.

There are lots of variations of this game. The basic process is to see how fast a class or several groups can come up with some factoids about each object. One method would be to divide into four teams. One group uses the library for their research, one group uses the internet. The other groups use a combination of sources, or perhaps get to choose which method of gathering data they think will work best.

Within a set time limit each group has to find out as much as possible about one or more of the objects in the collection. You might want to go a step further and have each group prepare a presentation (again explore the options for doing this: flip chart, one speaker, several speakers, PowerPoint presentation etc).

Once each group has presented their facts, you might want to explore if they thought their sources of information were reliable. And how much they may have cut and pasted or copied out without understanding the content.

45

Special Powers

Resources required: none.

Imagine that you have some amazing magical power that allows you to "see" memories contained in objects. Try to think yourself into the part with whatever props, magic words or superhero back story will help.

Simply go up to the object and see what impressions you can sense from the object (touching it may help to dramatise the process).

This can be an entertaining exercise in allowing a free flowing, stream of impressions and ideas.

46

Sounds of Discovery

Resources required: none, although musical instruments and other ways of making sounds make this game go with a bang!

For one or more of the objects, imagine the noises that were going on when it was discovered, that it made or that were around when it was created. The susurrations of the prehistoric sea that a trilobite might have heard, the clang of hammers as an ancient blade was forged, the sounds of plainsong as a medieval stone was being fixed into position within a church.

Try making these noises in some way.

47

Reuse, Recycle

Resources **required**: writing materials may help.

Consider how the objects in the collection could be reused, or used in different ways. The classic example of this is the use of a wire coat hanger as a car aerial. Could the man-made objects in the collection be repaired? What tools and materials would be needed? Could they be recycled in some way? Is there a difference between these objects and their contemporary equivalent? (For example, a wicker basket versus a plastic bag.) Discuss these ideas in small groups then report back to the larger group, perhaps with pictures illustrating your thoughts.

48

Love It or Hate It

Resources required: none.

A simple and useful process, especially if objects are being used in a self-exploratory or even therapeutic context.

Investigate the objects and then spend some time discussing which one(s) you like and why, and which other(s) you dislike and why. This can be the beginning of a number of illuminating conversations.

49

Designed For Life

Resources required: writing/drawing materials are useful.

Pick one or more of the objects in the collection and, working alone or in groups, design a new version of it. This could be an enhanced form of the object – either the modern version, or the older version using modern techniques and materials.

For example, how would a Victorian gas lamp look if it was still a gas lamp but used modern materials and styling? How would a ceramic hot water bottle look if you still used clay in its manufacture but coloured and styled the object in contemporary fashion? Alternatively, what if you still use clay in the manufacture but colour and style the object in contemporary fashion: how would it differ?

50

Sounding the Past

Resources required: sound recording equipment, computers with sound editing software.

Try exploring the sonic potential of your collections. Some objects may be tapped, fingers or even pencils run over them to generate sounds. Then there is the possibility of imagined noises, or sounds that an object can feedback from your own body. The most obvious example here is listening to the "sound of the sea" inside a shell. There are also sounds that could be associated with objects in the collection: the sound of horseshoes on the road, the sound of drunken singing with the harvest jug. Use digital recorders and free software available on the internet to produce some soundscapes. This game neatly combines imagination, investigative skills, information technology and music.

51

Visions and Voices

Resources required: writing/drawing materials (for storyboarding), craft materials for animation, lights, camera, action!

Developed from the idea of creating soundscapes, using simple digital equipment it is possible to animate objects from a collection. Adding eyes to an object (either with cut-out paper or in post-production on a computer) is the simplest way of bringing it to life. Sound effects can be added or conversations can be set up between different objects. One project I co-ordinated asked young people to record older members of their community, listening out in particular for people with strong local accents. These voices were synchronised with images by animating museum objects or by "claymation". Specialist skills are necessary for this kind of work, but creating Aardman-style *Creature Comforts* films using museum objects is far from impossible.

For a low-tech version of the same game, try creating a flickbook which shows the object(s) moving about. Now create a script to go with your visual story.

Space for Your Own Games

Object-Specific Games

The following are a few games designed to be used with particular types of object.

Containers

Certain objects in the collection will naturally suggest certain games. For example a "Treasure" Chest asks the question: what was once inside? The creation of treasure maps, verbal or written stories or poems about the chest's travels have lots of possibilities. Any vessel or container can become a magical receptacle: what can children imagine might come out of it? What is the first thing that they imagine (before they get any information about the object)? How do their ideas change as they get to know the object?

Them bones

Using bones, horns or other samples, can you imagine what animal they come from? If you have a skeleton or anatomical model to hand this can be a useful guide. How much information about an animal's habitat, diet and behaviour can we get from the specimen? If you want, you can discuss the techniques that palaeontologists use to find out where, when and how animals lived. What can't we see from bones? Think about non-boney structures like the trunk of an elephant or the comb of a chicken. What about the colours of an animal: can we make guesses based on the specimens we have, or the similarity between our specimen and animals we already know about?

Draw or make the animal you imagine.

Decoration

Look for decorative patterns, from milling on metals through to beadwork on ethnographic objects and scratched designs on sgraffito pottery. Encourage children to study the designs (a magnifying glass often helps). Try translating the patterns into different media, for example textiles or computer graphics.

Doors to other worlds

Door handles, keys, and hinges – all these things can be used as imaginative entrances to other worlds. Inspired by the object, what do the children imagine they would find? Ask them to write, draw or act out the new worlds they discover.

A similar exercise can be done with anything that can be looked through: portholes, telescopes, monocles – what do children imagine they could see?

Props

Any object could be used as a dramatic prop in a play. Obviously this may mean miming (or re-creating) the object itself if it's not suitable to be used directly.

Giving Objects a Context

The following games are designed to illustrate particular points in connection with how we interact with, care for, and understand objects.

Conservation challenge

This is a great way to engage with a real issue that faces museums and other collectors. There are a number of possible variations but the basic format is as follows:

- Take two objects – delicate things such as a blown chicken egg, a wasp's nest or a piece of sugar craft.
- Place one in a box, protected with tissue paper or bubble wrap.
- Take the other and pass it around the group. Allow the children to handle it.
- Compare the one that has been handled with the one in the box. How do they differ, has any damaged occurred to the one that has been handled?

This game extends naturally to a discussion of the balance between conservation and accessibility. If we don't want historic objects to be damaged, how should we pack, display, move and treat them? How important is it that an object can be touched?

More from less

This game can help children understand that sometimes having part of an object can actually tell us as much or even more about the past than the completed object.

The classic version of this game is given in Durbin, Morris and Wilkinson's *Learning from Objects* (1990):

- Prepare three boxes: one contains a complete china plate, the second half a plate and third one or more fragments of a shattered plate. All the plates should be identical.
- Three groups now examine the objects and see how much information they can find out.
- The groups then report their findings to the whole group. Point out that the group with the pottery fragments will be able to see the colour of the clay and understand something about how it fractures, whereas the group with the whole plate can't see the type of clay used.

A real puzzler

Find an object in your collection that you have no idea what it really is. Or an object which is missing any other information (such as an archaeological find that has no contextual data linked to it).

Discuss the issue of what information we should record with objects and how that information should be stored. Should we write on objects? Should we store information in a digital form and if so how do we ensure long-term preservation? Should we continue to use hand-written index descriptive cards and what problems might there be with this method? What about objects which are already in museum collections but we have little or no information about: should we still keep them? If we decide not to keep an object how should we dispose of it, and where?

Think Tank

The Think Tank is a unique service for schools from The Museum of Barnstaple and North Devon.

Using the Think Tank website teachers can select their own choice of museum objects for inclusion in a box that is delivered to their school. The website – www.museumthinktank.org.uk – includes pictures of the objects that are available and a few facts about each one for follow-up work. To date over 2000 children have made use of the Think Tank.

The Think Tank box is introduced by a film; then learners can explore the contents using a series of interactive games which are presented via a DVD.

The Think Tank has been developed by museum professionals and teachers to offer learners the chance to develop research, investigation and problem-solving skills that can be used across the curriculum. The Think Tank isn't about telling you what to think; it's about providing learners with an exciting environment in which they can develop their own thinking skills and strategies.

The Think Tank is suitable for learners from Year 3 onwards (but can be used with younger children when more support is offered) and for all ranges of ability. You can choose how long each game takes to play and can do as many as you want. Each Think Tank workshop last about 60 minutes.

To run the Think Tank you'll need a room with a DVD player (including speakers) and screen. You'll also need a few additional resources for some of the games (many of which are included in this book).

The Think Tank film has been designed so that it can be edited for use in other museums and contexts. If you are interested in adapting the Think Tank methodology for use with your collection, please contact the author at the following email address: Julian.Vayne@northdevon.gov.uk

Afterword

The world is full of objects. Things outside of us that link our inner subjective experience with the outer shared reality we all inhabit. By working with the wonderful things in museum collections we have a particularly rich resource for exploring ourselves and the world as it was, as it is and as it may become in the future.

I hope you find the suggestions in this book useful in building your own learning sessions. I'd be very interested in any feedback, ideas or observations you might discover from your own practice. Please feel free to drop me an email at: julian.vayne@gmail.com

About the Author

Julian Vayne works as a museum educator in the South West of England and is a passionate advocate of object-based learning. His *Museum Think Tank* project brought together museum objects and cutting-edge interactive film, winning a major award in 2008. He was also a key contributor to the 2011 award-winning *Sex and History* project with Exeter University and The Royal Albert Memorial Museum.

Introducing mindfulness practice into museums and using collections to support well-being and mental health is a major focus in his work, but he equally enjoys being the man from the museum who gets to show cool stuff to groups of school kids. He is an Associate of the Museums Association and is also a charitable trustee of the Friends of the Boscastle Museum of Witchcraft.

Index

Status 118-119

Also from MuseumsEtc

Interpretive Master Planning (Two Volumes)

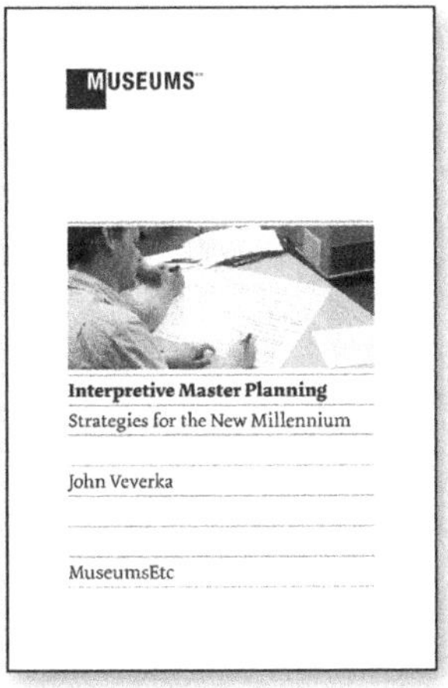

By John A Veverka

ISBN: 978-1-907697-23-4
and 978-1-907697-25-8 [paperback]
ISBN: 978-1-907697-24-1
and 978-1-907697-26-5 [hardback]

Order online
from www.museumsetc.com

Author John A Veverka is one of the world's leading consultants in interpretive planning, training and heritage tourism, with experience spanning over 30 years and taking him all over the world

Interpretive Master Planning presents - in two comprehensive volumes - a wealth of information on how to plan and design interpretive facilities and services.

John Veverka's lively text uses anecdotes, case histories and interactive examples to illustrate all aspects of interpretive planning: from theories of visitor psychology to budgeting, planning strategies and practical, field-tested ideas on everything from scriptwriting to evaluation.

This is the most comprehensive reference book on the subject, an invaluable resource for designing interpretation that really works.

"Here is knowledge based on years of national and international interpretive planning projects with parks, museums, commercial attractions and a variety of other agencies. This is a classic work by an author who does interpretive planning every day." Gary R Moore, Program Coordinator, MetroParks, Columbus and Franklin County, Ohio.

Creativity and Technology: Social Media, Mobiles and Museums

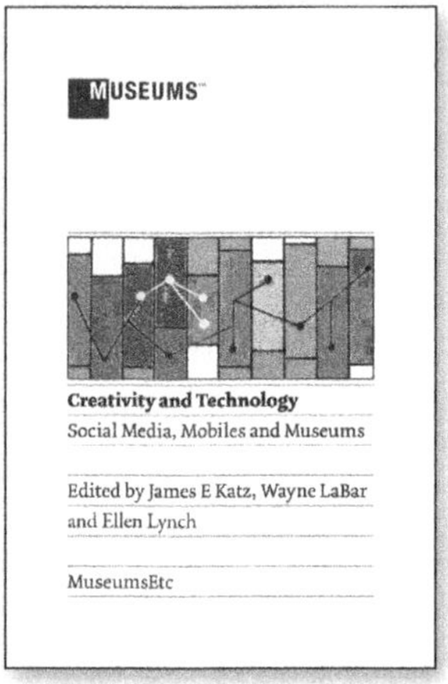

Editors: James E Katz, Wayne LaBar and Ellen Lynch

ISBN: 978-1-907697-11-1 [paperback]
ISBN: 978-1-907697-12-8 [hardback]

Order online from www.museumsetc.com

This book brings together papers given at a major conference organised by the Center for Mobile Communication Studies at Rutgers University (the world's first academic unit to focus solely on social aspects of mobile communication) and Liberty Science Center (the New Jersey-New York City region's largest education resource).

Presented by leading thinkers and museum experts, the papers provide an incisive, up-to-the-minute analysis of trends in the use of mobile devices by museum audiences, with a special focus on outreach efforts to under-served communities.

"This important collection of essays delves into a complex and exciting world, and makes a key contribution to this developing field." Dr. Lynda Kelly, Head of Web and Audience Research, Australian Museum, Sydney.

"Mobile technologies have the potential to revolutionize the museum experience. This book shares perspectives and findings that will help practitioners navigate this new learning terrain." Marsha Semmel, Deputy Director for Museums, Institute of Museum and Library Services, Washington DC.

Books

Academic Museums: Exhibitions and Education
Academic Museums: Beyond Exhibitions and Education
Alive To Change: Successful Museum Retailing
Contemporary Collecting: Theory and Practice
Conversations with Visitors: Social Media and Museums
Creating Bonds: Successful Museum Marketing
Creativity and Technology: Social Media, Mobiles and Museums
Inspiring Action: Museums and Social Change
Interpretive Master Planning: Philosophy, Theory and Practice
Interpretive Master Planning: Strategies for the New Millennium
Interpretive Planning Handbook
Museum Retailing: A Handbook of Strategies for Success
Museums and the Disposals Debate
Museums At Play: Games, Interaction and Learning
Narratives of Community: Museums and Ethnicity
New Thinking: Rules for the (R)evolution of Museums
Restaurants, Catering and Facility Rentals: Maximizing Earned Income
Rethinking Learning: Museums and Young People
Science Exhibitions: Communication and Evaluation
Science Exhibitions: Curation and Design
Social Design in Museums: The Psychology of Visitor Studies (2 volumes)
Sustainable Museums: Strategies for the 21st Century
The New Museum Community: Audiences, Challenges, Benefits
The Power of the Object: Museums and World War II
Twitter for Museums: Strategies and Tactics for Success

Videos

Cocktails and Culture: Cultivating Generation Next
Museums | Inclusion | Engagement
Planning and Designing for Children and Families
Real-World Twitter in Action

Order online at: www.museumsetc.com

Colophon

MuseumsEtc Ltd

Hudson House
8 Albany Street
Edinburgh EH1 3QB
UK

PO Box 425386
Cambridge
MA 02142
USA

www.museumsetc.com

ISBN: 978-1-907697-44-9

First published 2010
This edition first published 2012

The paper used in printing this book comes from responsibly managed forests and meets the requirements of the Forest Stewardship Council™ (FSC®) and the Sustainable Forestry Initiative® (SFI®). It is is acid free and lignin free and meets all ANSI standards for archival quality paper.

Typeset in Underware Dolly 10/16 and Adobe Myriad Pro 9/14.

A CIP catalogue record for this book is available from the British Library.

Lightning Source UK Ltd.
Milton Keynes UK
UKOW06f0918141215

264685UK00010B/162/P

9 781907 697449